THE CHINESE OPIUM-SMOKER

LECTOR HOUSE PUBLIC DOMAIN WORKS

THE CHINESE OPIUM-SMOKER

ANONYMOUS

ISBN: 978-93-5614-239-8

Published: -

LECTOR HOUSE LLP
E-MAIL: lectorpublishing@gmail.com

THE CHINESE OPIUM-SMOKER

TWELVE ILLUSTRATIONS
SHOWING THE RUIN WHICH OUR OPIUM TRADE
WITH CHINA IS BRINGING UPON
THAT COUNTRY.

Reproduced from the Chinese.

CONTENTS

I.

THE CHINESE OPIUM-SMOKER.
TWELVE ILLUSTRATIONS.

NO. 1.

THE incipient opium-smoker is reclining (as is usual) on a couch in his mansion, while his companion is indulging in tobacco through the water-pipe common in China.

NO. 2.

The opium-smoker, still portly and well-dressed, is entreated by his poor wife on bended knees to desist from the disastrous habit. His child is running off with the dreaded pipe; while the aged grandmother is seen coming, leaning on her staff, to add her tears and entreaties—now for the first time proved to be powerless. The hold of the pipe is already established; interest, duty, affection, reputation—all prove too feeble to arrest the downward career of the smoker. Sad indeed is the prospect; the husband is already doomed to poverty, shame, and an early grave; his wife to ruin, his child to beggary. His mother will die of a broken heart.

NO. 3.

Representing the progress in dissipation of the once sober gentleman, who has now, alas! become the victim of this vice. To him day has now become night, and night day. He can no longer sleep at night; and to banish the tedium of its long quiet hours, and to drown thought of the sure ruin awaiting him, becomes an absolute necessity. Regardless, therefore, alike of entreaty and censure, he now openly introduces into his house singing men and women, and gives himself up to their society. His books, formerly the companions of his choice, now lie unheeded on his table, and will not long retain even their place there. As for his poor family, powerless to prevent, or even retard, the downward progress of events, they can only consult their own safety by keeping altogether out of sight.

NO. 4.

ALL trace of literary occupation is now gone: the opium scales have taken the place of the classics. In the foreground a servant is preparing extract of opium, for crude opium is never smoked. Before the portable stove stands a small bucket of water, and a little charcoal lies on the ground beside it. The opium is boiled in water, and filtered; and the dregs are again boiled, till all the soluble matter is extracted. The watery solutions are then boiled down to the consistency of treacle, when it is ready for use.

At the table, by her husband, the wife of the smoker sits with pencil in hand, and with a long strip of paper before her. Now she needs to augment the family income. Happy is the wife who in these circumstances is able to execute Indian-ink drawings, or to write out ornamental quotations from the classics.

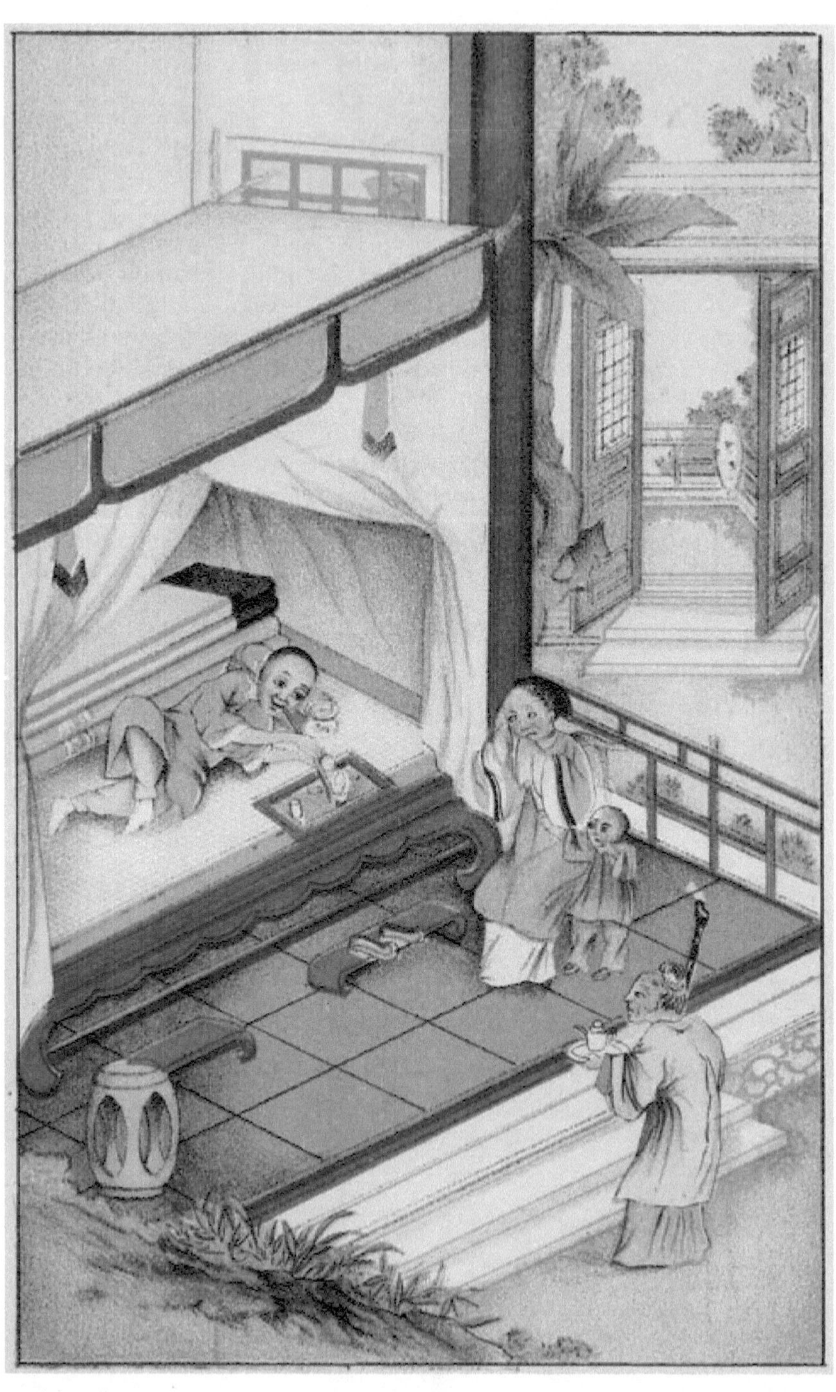

NO. 5.

Creditors will no longer forbear. Either the habit must at once and for ever be given up, or all hope of retaining possession of the ancestral property must be lost. The very graves of the ancestors join, as it were, in the last appeal of the weeping wife and mother, and of the weeping child, whose hopes of education, of literary advancement, and thus of promotion to office, are destroyed by the baneful narcotic.

The aged mother, now needing the support of a staff, is bringing hot tea for her son. Will he bring down *her* grey hairs with sorrow to the grave? Will he see her turned out, a homeless wanderer, out of the mansion in which she nursed and tended him when a helpless babe upon her lap?

NO. 6.

IT is easy to imagine the feelings of the unfortunate wife, who, seeing the misery and wretchedness wrought in her once comfortable home, determines to destroy the whole of the smoking apparatus. The tray and lamp are dashed upon the floor, a few more moments will see the destruction of the pipe itself; but the noise has reached the ears of her lord, who rushes in, and, forgetful of all the teachings of his great master, Confucius, proceeds to belabour her with the bamboo stick he has seized for the purpose, in spite of the cries of their unfortunate child. The entrance of an old and faithful retainer alone prevents him from inflicting serious injury.

NO. 7.

Still lower sinks the opium victim in his miserable career. The comfort and shelter of his paternal home are now things of the past. A roof which, from the absence of tiles, can hardly be said to cover, with at one side some bamboo matting to screen from the blast, and a mat, arranged to form a shelter, covering the place where meals, when forthcoming, may be cooked, is all that now remains to him of home. Surely he will see his folly, and give up the practice which has wrought him such ruin? *He cannot.* The appetite is perpetuated and intensified by that upon which it feeds. Without medical aid it would now probably be impossible to give up the habit, and indulgence in it has taken away all desire for assistance.

NO. 8.

Not much better than the shed in which he lives by day, is the shelter in which he now spends the night. Somewhat screened by the garden fence, his bed, supported at one end on a pile of bricks, at the other on his only remaining stool, is still covered by his curtains, and his opium lamp is sufficiently sheltered to keep alight. Most of his clothes have gone to the pawnshop; ere long his curtains will follow them. His wife and child, the picture of misery, can only look with hopeless sorrow on the living and half-naked skeleton of the once portly and well-dressed gentleman. Wealth and property have gone, clothes and respectability have gone, home and health have gone, and what remains? Ah, what indeed! There is a ruined soul in that poor, heartless, wrecked body, almost beyond the possibility of salvation.

NO. 9.

The victim of opium is now a homeless beggar, squatting in some out-of-the-way corner, and dependent upon charity for a morsel of bread. His unshaven head well agrees with the general squalor of his appearance, and the ground is now his only bed and table. His sole remaining possessions are his opium-pipe and a few earthenware cooking utensils. Some compassionate person, perhaps a former farm-servant, is bringing him a small flattened loaf.

NO. 10.

Crime too often follows the destitution caused by opium-smoking; for *at all costs* opium *must* be had. Thefts, robberies, or even murders may result. The wretched culprit may have to flee from justice, or to make his escape from a neighbourhood which will no longer tolerate him. The very dogs pursue him. Probably the bucket in which the wanderer carries his pipe, and the labourer's hat slung behind him, are both stolen. Some cave among the hills may shelter him, or the rocks may shield him from the cutting wind.

NO. 11.

THE downward course of the opium-smoker is now very rapid. Exposure to the weather and want of food accelerate the injurious effects of the opium. No one would think of giving a night's shelter to a man whose imperious craving for opium would compel him to rob his benefactor before morning. Endeavouring to warm himself in the sunshine, with unshaven head and haggard countenance, the sower coming with his seed-basket finds him in a sheltered corner of the field.

NO. 12.

Winter draws on apace. The fields supply nothing that the wretched opium-smoker can eat. All he can beg is insufficient to purchase that opium without which he could not exist for a single day; he has therefore exchanged his only shirt for a little opium, to quiet for a time what an opium-smoker well called "the torments of the hell within." All power of enjoyment has long since passed away: now there is nothing before him but suffering—suffering beyond the grave! With trembling steps and a shivering frame he seeks the shelter of a cave among the rocks, in which he will lie down and *die*. Nor is he alone in his misery; thousands of similar victims are living, dying, dead—they are to be found everywhere.

II.

OPIUM-SMOKING IN CHINA COMPARED WITH THE DRINKING HABITS OF ENGLAND.

On this point the evidence of Mr. (now Sir Thomas) Wade, K.C.B., Her Majesty's minister at the Court of Peking, given in Government Blue Book, No. 5 (1871), p. 432, is so decisive, that it precludes the necessity of further testimony. He says:—

"It is to me vain to think otherwise of the use of the drug in China, than as of a habit many times more pernicious, nationally speaking, than the gin and whisky drinking which we deplore at home. It takes possession more insidiously, and keeps its hold to the full as tenaciously. I know no case of radical cure. It has insured in every case within my knowledge the steady descent, moral and physical, of the smoker, and it is so far a greater mischief than drink, that it does not, by external evidence of its effect, expose its victim to the loss of repute which is the penalty of habitual drunkenness."

III.

THE EXTENT OF OPIUM-SMOKING IN CHINA.

In the absence of an official census, we can only select the most reliable evidence to be had on the subject.

J. Dudgeon, Esq., M.D., C.M., of the Peking Mission Hospital, estimates that of the male population in China generally, probably 30 to 40 per cent. smoke opium; of the general city population, 40 to 60 per cent.

The former of these statements is perhaps rather excessive, seeing that the same authority gives the number of agriculturists and field labourers as averaging only 4 to 6 per cent.

Of the city population we have from various quarters more minute estimates to guide us.

Taking three important cities from various parts of the country, we find that the number of opium-smokers does in each case exceed the estimate given by Dr. Dudgeon.

1.—Suchow, the capital of the province of Kiang Su. The Rev. C. H. Du Bose, a resident missionary, writes:—"As a minimum estimate, seven-tenths of the adult males smoke opium. To this fact all of the natives you ask will attest."

2.—Ningpo, a city of 400,000 inhabitants in the province of Chekiang.

"It contains 2,700 opium-shops, or a shop for every 148 inhabitants, or every thirty men."

(*v. Mander's "Our Opium Trade with China," p. 8.*)

3.—Tai Yuen, the capital of the province of Shansi. A resident missionary writes:—

"It is estimated that six or seven out of every ten men you meet are addicted to the habit of opium-smoking, and a larger proportion of women than I have seen in any other city. There are about 400 retail opium-shops, and seventy or eighty wholesale dealers."

It is probable that these cities exceed the average number of opium-smokers throughout the city population in China; indeed, had not the number been extraordinary, the estimate would probably not have been made, but if the number be reduced by one-half, we have still 30 per cent. of the city population through-out China—in other words, some tens of millions—who are the slaves of the opium-pipe.

IV.

ENGLAND'S RESPONSIBILITY IN REGARD TO THE CHINESE OPIUM-SMOKER.

SUMMARY of facts bearing upon the relation of Great Britain to the Chinese opium-trade:—

1.—When China, as a nation, knew nothing of the vice of opium-smoking, British merchants introduced the drug, enriching the treasury of the East India Company to the demoralisation of the Chinese nation.

2.—When the Chinese Government vigorously remonstrated and strenuously opposed, England carried the legalisation of the trade at the point of the sword.

3.—When the Chinese, discomfited in the field, appealed to the generosity and humanity of the British Government for the suppression of the trade, the British Government continued and upheld the policy they had inaugurated by force of arms.

4.—When the subject is brought before the Houses of Parliament, the trade is acknowledged to be unjustifiable, yet, because of the revenue it brings to the Indian empire, and the difficulties surrounding Indian finance, it is upheld by the Government and supported by the Opposition.

Lector House believes that a society develops through a two-fold approach of continuous learning and adaptation, which is derived from the study of classic literary works spread across the historic timeline of literature records. Therefore, we aim at reviving, repairing and redeveloping all those inaccessible or damaged but historically as well as culturally important literature across subjects so that the future generations may have an opportunity to study and learn from past works to embark upon a journey of creating a better future.

This book is a result of an effort made by Lector House towards making a contribution to the preservation and repair of original ancient works which might hold historical significance to the approach of continuous learning across subjects.

HAPPY READING & LEARNING!

LECTOR HOUSE LLP
E-MAIL: lectorpublishing@gmail.com